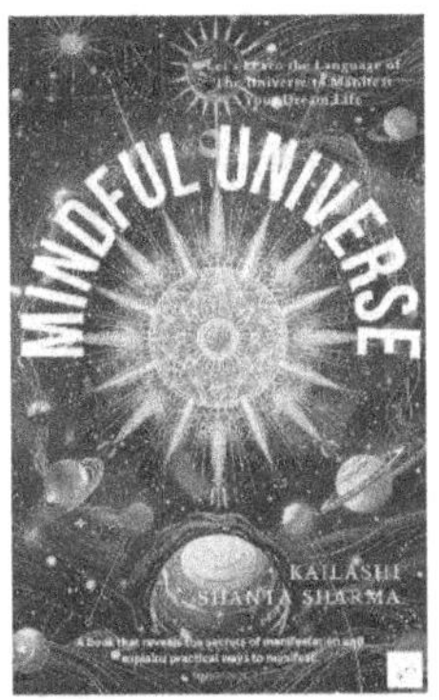

MINDFUL UNIVERSE

Let's Learn the Language of
The Universe to Manifest
Your Dream Life

SHANTA SHARMA

DIRECTOR

KAILASHI GLOBAL PUBLICATIONS
BHARAT
kailashigp@gmail.com

Kailashi Global Publications Pvt. Ltd., Bharat

MINDFUL UNIVERSE

PUBLISHER: SHANTA SHARMA

36 VASANT VIHAR

GOVERDHAN VILAS SECTOR 14, UDAIPUR, RAJ.

WRITER: KAILASHI SHANTA SHARMA

SELLER: AMAZON, D2D, Notion Press India etc.

FIRST EDITION: MARCH 2024

Email- kailashigp@gmail.com

Content

1. **QUANTUM SELF-AWARENESS**
   How to use quantum physics and neuroscience to understand the nature of reality.

2. **HARMONIC ALIGNMENT**
   How to align your thoughts, emotions, and actions with the frequency of desired outcomes.

3. **CREATIVE CONSCIOUSNESS**
   How to tap into the infinite intelligence and creative power of the universe mind.

4. **EMPOWER SELF-BELIEF**
   How to overcome limiting beliefs, fears, and negative patterns that block manifestation abilities.

5. **INNER HARMONY**
   How to practice mindfulness, meditation, and visualization to enhance connection with the universe.

6. **MANIFESTING INTENTIONS**
   How to apply the law of attraction, the law of vibration, and other universal laws to attract what you want in life.

7. **ENHANCED MANIFESTATION**
   How to use gratitude, affirmations, and intention to amplify manifestation power.

8. **TAILORED MANIFESTATION**
   How to create a personalized manifestation plan that suits your goals, personality, and lifestyle.

9. **UNIVERSE FEEDBACK**
   How to recognize and interpret the signals, synchronicities, and feedback from the universe.

10. **JOYFUL GROWTH**
    How to celebrate success, learn from failures, and enjoy the journey of manifesting the dream life.

Why to Read Mindful Universe....?

Do you want to learn how to manifest your dream life by decoding the language of the universe?

Do you want to discover the secrets of quantum physics, neuroscience, and spirituality that can help you understand the nature of reality and your role in it?

Do you want to tap into the infinite intelligence and creative power of the universe's mind and enjoy the life you want?

If you answer yes, to any of these questions, then this book is for you. ***Mindful Universe*** is a comprehensive and practical guide that will teach you how to use **the principles and techniques of manifestation to create and attract the desired reality.**

In this book, you will learn how to-

- **Align your thoughts**, emotions, and actions with the frequency of your desired outcomes
- **Attract your desired outcomes** from the quantum field and the universe mind
- **Allow your desired outcomes to manifest** in your physical reality and life
- **Overcome your limiting beliefs,** fears, and negative patterns that block your manifestation abilities

- **Practice mindfulness,** meditation, and visualization to enhance your connection with the universe
- **Apply the law of attraction,** the law of vibration, and other universal laws to attract what you want in life
- **Recognize and interpret** the signals, synchronicities, and feedback from the universe
- **Celebrate your success,** learn from your failures, and enjoy the journey of manifesting your dream life

Mindful Universe is more than just a book. It is a transformational tool that will empower you to become the master of your destiny. **By reading and applying the teachings of this book, you will be able to access your inner wisdom, and creativity and manifest your dream life.**

The universe is mindful. Every creation exists for a cause. Unless and until the cause matches its frequency with the creator, it will suffer.

As and when it tunes to the desired frequency, regardless of time and space, it manifests.

- **Kailashi Shanta D.**

Foreword

Have you ever wondered how the universe works, and how you can use its secrets to create your dream life?

Have you ever felt that there is more than reality what you see, hear, or touch and that you have a deeper connection with the source of all creation and intelligence?

Have you ever wanted to tap the infinite wisdom and creativity of the universe mind, and enjoy the life you want?

If you answered yes, to any of these questions, then you are here for a treat. ***Mindful Universe*** is a book that will open somewhat your eyes, mind, and heart to the wonders and mysteries of the universe, <u>and show you how to use its language to manifest your desires.</u> ***Mindful Universe*** is a book that will teach you how to use the principles and techniques of quantum physics, neuroscience, and spirituality to understand the nature of reality and your role in it. ***Mindful Universe*** is a book that will help you align your thoughts, emotions, and actions with the frequency of your desired outcomes, and attract them from the quantum field and the universe mind.

Mindful Universe is not just a book. It is a journey of discovery, transformation, and empowerment. ***<u>It is a journey that will take you from the realm of the physical and material life to the realm of the metaphysical and spiritual life. It is a journey that</u>***

will take you from the realm of the finite and limited to the realm of the infinite and unlimited. It is a journey that will take you from the realm of the ego and separation to the realm of the soul and unity.

Kailashi

Shanta Sharma

Director KGPB

1

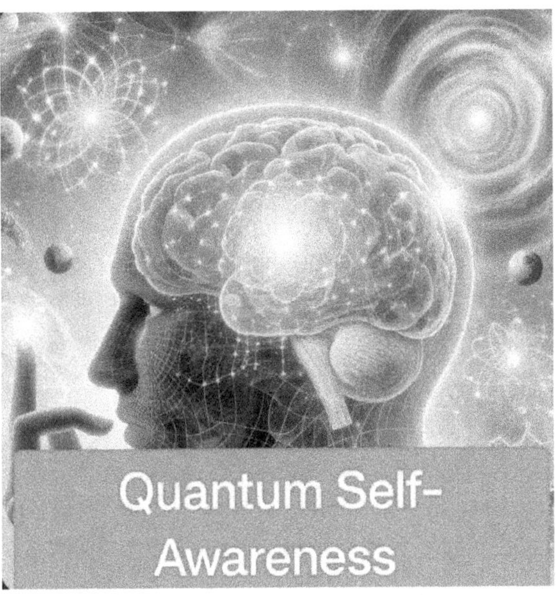

How to use quantum physics and neuroscience to understand the nature of reality

Quantum physics and neuroscience are two different fields of science that study different aspects of reality.

Quantum physics is the branch of physics that deals with the behaviour and interactions of the smallest particles and waves of matter and energy, such as electrons, photons, and atoms.

Neuroscience is the branch of biology that studies the structure and function of the nervous system, especially the brain, and its relation to behaviour and cognition.

Quantum physics and neuroscience are both very complex and fascinating subjects, but they are not directly comparable. However, some researchers have proposed that quantum physics may have some implications for neuroscience and psychology, especially for the understanding of consciousness. For example, some hypotheses suggest that quantum phenomena, such as entanglement and superposition, may play a role in the brain's information processing and may explain some aspects of consciousness that are not accounted for by classical physics (1,2). These hypotheses are collectively known as **quantum mind theories** (3).

However, quantum mind theories are not widely accepted by the mainstream scientific community, as they face many challenges and criticisms, such as the lack of empirical evidence, the difficulty of testing and falsifying them, and the problem of explaining how quantum effects can be maintained in the warm and noisy environment of the brain (2). Therefore, quantum physics and neuroscience remain largely separate domains of inquiry, with different methods, assumptions, and goals.

Reality is not what it seems. It is not a fixed and objective thing that exists independently of our perception. Rather, it is a dynamic and subjective phenomenon that emerges from the interaction of our mind and the physical world. In this chapter, we will explore how quantum physics and neuroscience can help and understand the nature of reality and our role in it.

 Quantum physics: the science of possibilities

Quantum physics is the branch of physics that deals with the behaviour and interactions of the smallest particles and waves of matter and energy, such as electrons, photons, and atoms. Quantum physics reveals that the **physical world is not deterministic, but probabilistic.** This means that the outcome of any physical event is not predetermined, but depends on the observation and measurement of it. For example, an electron can exist in a superposition of two or more states, such as being in two places at one time, until it is observed and collapses into one definite state.

Quantum physics also reveals that **the physical world is not local, but nonlocal. <u>This means that the state of one particle can affect the state of another particle, even if they are separated by a large distance, without any physical connection or communication</u>.** This phenomenon is known as **quantum entanglement**- For example, two entangled photons can have opposite polarizations, such as vertical and horizontal, and if one photon is measured and found to have a vertical polarization, the other photon will instantly have a horizontal polarization, regardless of how far apart they are.

Quantum physics challenges our common sense and classical view of reality, which assumes that reality is objective, deterministic, and local. Quantum physics suggests that reality is subjective, probabilistic, and nonlocal. *Quantum physics implies that reality is not a fixed and solid thing, but a fluid and flexible thing, that depends on our observation and participation. Quantum physics implies that reality is not a single and absolute thing, but a multiple and relative thing, that reflects our perspective and intention. Quantum physics implies that reality is not a separate and isolated thing, but a connected and holistic thing, that responds to our influence and interaction.*

Neuroscience: the science of perception

Neuroscience is the branch of biology that studies the structure and function of the nervous system, especially the brain, and its relation to behaviour and cognition. **Neuroscience reveals that the brain is not a passive and faithful receiver of reality, but an active and creative constructor of reality.** The brain does not simply record and reproduce the sensory input from the external world, **but rather filters, interprets, and transforms it according to its internal models, memories, and expectations.**

Neuroscience also reveals that the brain is not a single and unified entity, but a complex and diverse network of specialized regions, circuits, and cells. The brain consists of different levels of the organization, from molecules to neurons to synapses to networks to systems, that interact and communicate with each other in various ways. The brain also consists of different modes of operation, such as conscious and unconscious, rational and emotional, analytical and intuitive, that influence and balance each other in various situations.

Neuroscience challenges our naive and simplistic view of perception, which assumes that **perception** is direct, accurate, and complete. Neuroscience suggests that **perception is indirect, approximate, and incomplete. Neuroscience implies that perception is not a fixed and static process, but a dynamic and adaptive process, that depends on our attention and learning.** Neuroscience implies that perception is not a single and uniform process, but a multiple and diverse process, **that reflects our individuality and variability.** Neuroscience implies that perception is not a separate and independent process, but **a connected and interdependent process and is affected by our cognition and emotion.**

Reality

Reality is the product of mind and matter. It is not something that exists, but something that emerges from the interaction of our mind and the physical world. Quantum physics and neuroscience can help us to understand the nature of reality and our role in it. Quantum physics can help us to understand the nature of the physical world and how it responds to our observation and participation. Neuroscience can help us understand the nature of our mind and how it constructs and influences our perception and experience of reality.

By understanding the nature of reality and our role in it, we can also learn how to shape and change it. *We can learn how to use our mind to affect the physical world, and how to use the physical world to affect our mind*. <u>*We can learn how to use quantum physics and neuroscience to manifest our dream life.*</u>

How to manifest your dream life

Manifesting your dream life is the process of creating and attracting the reality that you desire. It is based on the idea that your thoughts, emotions, and actions have a direct impact on the physical world and the physical world provides direct feedback to your thoughts, emotions, and actions. Manifesting your dream life involves three steps: **aligning, attracting, and allowing (AAA).**

Aligning

It is a step of aligning your thoughts, emotions, and actions with the frequency of your desired outcomes. It is based on the idea that **everything in the universe, including you and your reality, is made of energy and vibration, and that like attracts like.** Unless and until your frequency does not match your desired frequency, you can't attract that. You need to be vibrant enough as per your desired goal. We never receive what we desire but what we deserve. If one deserves, the universe delivers without any desire.

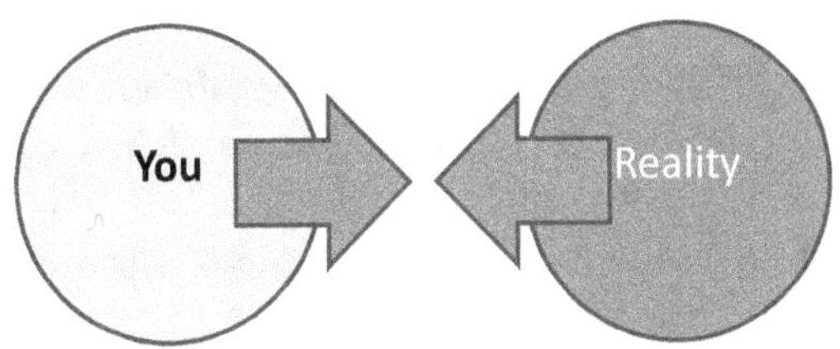

To align with your desired outcomes, you need to apply the **VFA formula**, explained below-

Visualize (V)

Visualize your desired outcomes in vivid and specific detail, as if they are already happening in the present moment. This will activate the same brain regions and neural pathways that are involved in the experience of your desired outcomes, and create a mental blueprint of it.

Feel (F)

Feel the positive emotions that are associated with your desired outcomes, such as joy, gratitude, love, and excitement. This will generate the same **biochemical and hormonal signals** that are involved in the experience of your desired outcomes, and **create an emotional magnet** for it.

Act(A)

Act as if your desired outcomes are already true and inevitable, and take **inspired and consistent actions** that are aligned with them. This will demonstrate your **faith and commitment** to your desired outcomes, and create physical evidence for them.

By aligning your thoughts, emotions, and actions with the frequency of your desired outcomes, you will create coherent and powerful signals that will resonate with the quantum field and the universe mind and will initiate the process of manifestation.

Attracting

It is a step of attracting your desired outcomes from the quantum field and the universe mind. It is based on the idea that the quantum field and the universe mind are the source of all possibilities and intelligence and that they respond to your signals and intentions. To attract your desired outcomes, you need to apply the **ABR formula**, explained below-

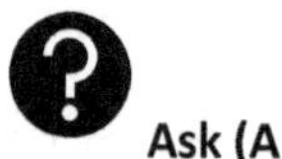

Ask (A)

Ask for your desired outcomes with clarity and confidence, and express your intention to the quantum field and the universe's mind. This will activate the **law of attraction**, which states that whatever you ask for, you will receive.

 **Believe (B)**

Believe that your desired outcomes are possible and available, and trust that the quantum field and the universe mind will deliver them to you. This will activate the **law of vibration**, which states that whatever you believe, you will attract.

 **Receive (R)**

Receive the signs, synchronicities, and feedback from the quantum field and the universe mind, and acknowledge and appreciate them. This will activate the law of gratitude, which states that whatever you are grateful for, will multiply your desired outcomes.

By attracting your desired outcomes from the quantum field and the universe mind, you will **create a connection and communication with the source of all creation and intelligence, and accelerate the process of manifestation.**

Allowing

It is a step of allowing your desired outcomes to manifest in your physical reality. It is based on the idea that your physical reality is the result of your observation and measurement and that it reflects your perception and expectation. To allow your desired outcomes to manifest, you need to apply the **DEC formula** explained below-

Detach (D)

Detach from the outcome and the timing, and release any attachment and resistance to your desired outcomes. This will activate the **law of detachment**, *which states that whatever you let go of, you will receive.*

Expectations (E)

Expect the best, and cultivate an optimistic attitude towards your desired outcomes. This will activate the **law of expectation**, which states that *whatever you expect, you will experience*.

Celebration (C)

Celebrate your success, learn from your failures, and enjoy the journey and the process of manifestation. This will activate the **law of joy**, which states that *whatever you celebrate, you will increase celebrations*.

By allowing your desired outcomes to manifest in your physical reality, you will create harmony and congruence between your inner and outer world, and complete the process of manifestation.

Conclusion

Reality is the product of mind and matter. Quantum physics and neuroscience can help us to understand the nature of reality and our role in it. By understanding the nature of reality and our role in it, we can learn how to shape and change it. We can learn how to use quantum physics and neuroscience together to manifest our dream life. Manifesting our dream life involves three steps: aligning, attracting, and allowing. By following these steps, we can create and attract the reality that we desire and can live our dream life.

Manifestation and the Seasons: A Metaphorical Connection

Manifestation

Manifestation refers to the process of bringing our desires, intentions, or goals into reality. It involves aligning our thoughts, emotions, and actions to attract what we want.

Just like the changing seasons, where nature transitions from one phase to another, our manifestations also follow a natural rhythm. All earthlings receive according to their eligibility and requirements, except humans. Only humans can enjoy ultimate pleasure, as humans can enhance their eligibility. Naturally, we cannot get apples from a Neem tree, but in the case of humans, it's not so. Humans can do anything just by tuning frequency with the universal mind or mooting.

Our true problem is that we know that we can do what we desire and deserve. Our problem is that we cannot sit waiting for the time/season to fulfill our desires. That's why we focus on our skills, improve ourselves, resonate our frequency with the universe, tune ourselves, control our emotions, and work hard consistently. We try to understand universal law and try hard to get apples from a Neem tree, as through manifestation nothing is impossible. And ultimately, we win because we moot.

The Season Theorem (Metaphor)

It always takes some time for the universe to deliver what we desire and deserve, just like the seasons. But in a few cases, we receive it immediately or without desire, just like the weather.

Imagine that our desires are seeds we plant in the soil of our consciousness.

Spring

During spring, seeds sprout and new life emerges. Similarly, when we set intentions, we plant the seeds of manifestation.

Summer

In summer, plants grow vigorously, fuelled by sunlight and warmth. Similarly, our intentions gain momentum as we focus on them consistently.

Autumn (Fall)

Autumn brings harvest. We reap what we've sown. Similarly, our manifestations start materializing.

Winter

Winter is a time of rest and reflection. It's when we trust that what we've planted will continue to grow beneath the surface, even if it's not visible. Similarly, patience and trust are essential during the manifestation process.

Weather Formulas (Symbolic)

Temperature

Represents our emotional state. When we're aligned and positive, the "temperature" is warm, aiding manifestation.

Pressure

Symbolizes our mental focus. High pressure (clarity) supports manifestation, while low pressure (doubt) hinders it.

Wind

Signifies action. Consistent effort (gentle breeze) propels manifestations, while stagnation (calm air) delays them.

Humidity

Reflects receptivity. High humidity (openness) allows manifestations to flow, while low humidity (resistance) creates obstacles.

Precipitation

Represents results. Positive thoughts and actions lead to fruitful outcomes (rain), while negativity yields drought.

Real-Life Application

Just as seasons change gradually, manifestations unfold over time. Some desires manifest quickly (like spring flowers), while others take longer (like fruit-bearing trees).

Factors like alignment, consistency, and trust influence the speed of manifestation.

Remember that unseen growth occurs even during the "winter" of waiting.

In summary, our manifestations align with the natural cycles of seasons. Trust the process, nurture your intentions, and allow time for the seeds you've planted to bloom.

Learning by doing

Learning by doing, or an experience-driven approach is based on the idea that learning occurs through direct engagement with the environment, tasks, or problems. This approach can foster active, hands-on, and authentic learning experiences that can enhance motivation, creativity, and problem-solving skills. It can also help learners develop a deeper understanding of the concepts and principals involved, as well as their applications and implications. However, this approach can also pose some challenges, such as requiring more time, resources, and guidance from the instructor or facilitator. It can also lead to misconceptions, errors, or frustration if the learners lack the necessary prior knowledge, skills, or feedback to perform the tasks or solve the problems.

Doing after learning

Doing after learning, or a knowledge-driven approach, is based on the idea that learning occurs through acquiring and processing information from various sources, such as lectures, books, or videos. This approach can provide learners with a systematic, structured, and comprehensive overview of the subject matter, as well as the relevant theories, facts, and rules. It can also help learners acquire the foundational knowledge and skills that are essential for further learning and application. However, this approach can also have some drawbacks, such as being passive, abstract, and detached from the real-world context. It can also result in superficial or rote learning, where learners memorize the information without understanding or applying it.

Therefore, the best approach to learning may depend on various factors, such as the learner's characteristics, preferences, and goals; the instructor's role and expectations; the subject matter and its complexity; and the learning environment and its resources. Ideally, a balanced and integrated approach that combines both learning by doing and doing after learning can be more effective and engaging than either approach alone. Such an approach can allow learners to benefit from both the experiential and the informational aspects of learning, and to achieve a deeper and more meaningful learning outcome.

You can do whatever you want.

First of all, decide what you want to do.

Your goal should appear to you as clear as glass.

Once you have set your goal, stick to it.

Now, with complete honesty, self-assess your eligibility and suitability to achieve your goal.

If there are slight deficiencies, you can improve your skills with your thoughts, emotions, hard work and determination and send the message of your dedication towards the goal to the universe. This is the stage when you match your current lower frequency with the higher frequency you desire to achieve.

Only humans can do this in the entire universe. Refinement of thoughts is possible through contemplation and many sages have proved this.

You will find that just by developing yourself and resolving to improve your abilities, every part of your being will become active. This will send a message to the entire universe through which all the powers will help you in achieving your goal. You make yourself active by refining your goal with your emotions and the entire universe becomes supportive in achieving your small goal. By your action, you turn the odds in your favour.

Here your struggle is with yourself. You are the doer; you are the sustainer. Negative forces try to discourage you every moment, but you remain alert and fight the external and internal negative forces. Best wishes to you in advance that by remaining firm and steadfast, you have activated every pore of your being to achieve your desired goal.

When you are active, many obstacles, and momentary apprehensions (can't happen, impossible, turn back, reduce the target, etc.) start coming in front of you. But you should be alert and keep your focus on your goal and do not let a layer of doubts cloud it. This is the time to test your dedication to your goal, faith in your abilities, and faith in the cosmic powers.

It may take time to achieve your goal. Even though everything in nature is predetermined, everything appears to be random. It is already decided that if a mango tree is planted then only mangoes will grow on it. But this is not possible in nature before the season arrives. No matter how favourable the weather may be, one still has to wait, for this natural event to occur. Similarly, it may take time to achieve your goal. Four different situations of goal manifestation are possible -

- Manifestation without asking - without resolution
- Manifestation by mere resolution without asking
- Manifestation takes place by asking, by resolution

- Manifestation takes place by asking, by resolution and by actively optimizing one's ability.

MANIFESTATION IS A MUST (AS IN THE CASE OF HUMANS- FRUIT NEVER DEPENDS UPON ROOT)

ALIGNING (IMAGIN- WHAT YOU WANT TO BE)

ATTRACTING (CHECK ELIGIBILITY-INNER SELF CERTIFICATION) (IF FAILS WORK HARD ON YOUR EMOTIONS, SKILLS AND ATTITUDE TO TUNE WITH THE DESIRED FREQUENCY)

ALLOWING YOURSELF TO FEEL IT (FEEL IT TO BE IT)

TIME ISSUE (SEASON THEOREM AND WEATHER F

ORMULA)

THE UNIVERSE IS MINDFUL- EVERYONE RECEIVES WHAT HE DESERVES, RESERVES AND CONSERVES

IN THE CASE OF HUMANS, THE FRUITS NEVER DEPEND ON THE ROOTS BUT ON HOW ONE MOOTS.

Books-

Greene, B. (2005) The fabric of the cosmos: Space, time, and the texture of reality. New York: Vintage Books

Radin, D. (2006) Entangled minds: Extrasensory experiences in a quantum reality. New York: Paraview Pocket Books

Aspect, A., Dalibard, J., & Roger, G. (1982) Experimental test of Bell's inequalities using time-varying analyzers. Physical Review Letters, 49(25)

References-

1. https://scienceandnonduality.com
2. www.physics.ili.gov
3. https://en.wikipedia.org
4. https://link.springer.com

2

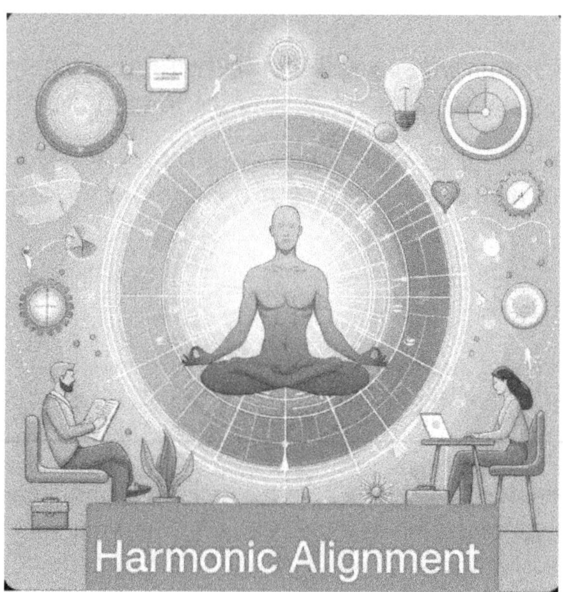

How to align your thoughts, emotions, and actions with the frequency of your desired outcome

One of the key steps to manifest your dream life is to align your thoughts, emotions, and actions with the frequency of your desired outcome.

Frequency is the rate at which something vibrates or oscillates, and determines the nature and quality of energy. **Everything in the universe, including you and your reality, is made of energy and vibration, and like attracts like.** This means that whatever frequency you emit, you will attract the same frequency back. Therefore, to attract the desired reality, you need to align your frequency with it **by your thoughts, feelings, and actions.**

How to align your thoughts

Your thoughts are powerful tools that can shape your reality. Your thoughts create your beliefs and your beliefs create your expectations, which further create your experiences. Your thoughts also affect your emotions, which in turn affect your actions. Therefore, to align your thoughts with the frequency of your desired outcome, you need to **think positively, specifically and consistently.**

**Think positively**

Thinking positively means focusing on the good aspects of yourself, your life, and your reality and avoiding negative thoughts that bring you low. Positive thinking can help you **raise your vibration, boost your confidence, and attract more positive experiences.** To think positively, you can use **affirmations, gratitude, and optimism.**

**Think specifically**

Thinking specifically means having a clear, precise but detailed vision of what you want to manifest, and why you want to manifest it. Specific thinking can help you create **a mental blueprint** for your desired outcome and activate the law of attraction. To think specifically, you can use **visualization, goal-setting, and intention.**

Think consistently

Thinking consistently means maintaining your positive and specific thoughts throughout this journey and **avoiding distractions and doubts** that may interfere with your manifestation. Consistent thinking can help you <u>**create a coherent and powerful signal that resonates with the quantum field and the universal mind.**</u> To think consistently, you can practice repetition, focus, and meditation.

By aligning your thoughts with the frequency of your desired outcome, you will create a strong and clear mental impression that will attract the corresponding physical manifestation.

How to align your emotions

Your emotions are powerful indicators that can guide your reality. **Your emotions reflect your inner state, your vibration, and your alignment with your true self.** Your emotions also affect your thoughts, which in turn affect your actions. Therefore, to align your emotions with the frequency of your desired outcomes, you need to **feel positively, specifically, and consistently.**

 **Feel positively**

Feeling positive means experiencing the positive emotions that are associated with your desired outcome such as joy, love, gratitude, and excitement. **Positive feelings can help you raise your vibration, enhance your attraction, and amplify your manifestation.** To feel positive, you can use **appreciation, celebration, and compassion.**

 **Feel specifically**

Feeling specifically means generating the same emotions that you would feel if your desired outcome were already true and inevitable, and matching them with your thoughts and actions. Specific feelings can help you **create an emotional magnet for your desired outcome and activate the law of vibration.** To feel specific, you can use **emotion, imagination, and embodiment.**

 **Feel consistently**

Feeling consistently means sustaining your positive and specific emotions throughout the journey and avoiding emotions and moods that may lower your vibration or misalign you with your desired outcome. Consistent feeling can help you **create harmony and congruence between your inner and outer world,**

and accelerate your manifestation. To feel consistently, you can use **awareness, regulation, and expression.**

By aligning your emotions with the frequency of your desired outcome, you will create a strong and clear emotional connection that will attract corresponding physical manifestation.

How to align your actions

Your actions are powerful catalysts that can transform your reality. But there is no attraction without action. Your actions demonstrate your faith, commitment, and readiness for your desired outcome. Your actions also affect your thoughts, which in turn affect your emotions. Therefore, to align your actions with the frequency of your desired outcome you need to **act positively, specifically, and consistently.**

🚀 Act positively

Acting positively means taking actions that are aligned with your positive thoughts and emotions, and avoiding actions that are contrary to them. **Positive actions can help you raise your vibration, increase your confidence, and attract more positive opportunities**. To act positively, you can **use courage, integrity, and generosity.**

 **Act specifically**

Acting specifically means taking actions that are aligned with your specific thoughts and emotions, and matching them with your desired outcome. Specific action can help you **create a piece of physical evidence for your desired outcome and activate the law of action.** To act specifically, you can follow **planning, execution, and feedback.**

 **Act consistently**

Acting consistently means taking actions that are aligned with your consistent thoughts and emotions and maintaining them throughout your journey. Consistent action can help you **create momentum and habit for your desired outcome and accelerate your manifestation.** To act consistently, you can practice **discipline, persistence, and improvement.**

By aligning your actions with the frequency of your desired outcome you will create a strong and clear physical expression that will attract corresponding physical manifestation.

Conclusion

Aligning your thoughts, emotions, and actions with the frequency of your desired outcome is one of the key steps to manifest your dream life. By aligning your frequency with your desired outcomes, you will **create a coherent and powerful signal that will resonate with the quantum field and the universal** mind, and initiate the process of manifestation. To align your frequency with your desired outcome you need to think, feel, and act positively, specifically, and consistently. By following these steps, you can create and attract the reality that you desire, and thus live your dream life.

AAA

You can apply these principles to your life by following the three steps of manifestation: **aligning, attracting, and allowing.** You can start by choosing a specific goal or outcome that you want to manifest, and then-

Align your thoughts, emotions, and actions with the frequency of your desired outcome. Visualize, feel, and act as if it is already true and inevitable.

Attract your desired outcome from the quantum field and the universal mind. Ask, believe, and receive the signs, synchronicities, and feedback from the source of all creation and intelligence.

Allow your desired outcome to manifest in your physical reality. Detach from the outcome and the timing, expect the best, celebrate your success and learn from your failures.

By applying these principles in your life, you can create and attract the reality that you desire and live your dream life.

What Stops You?

Resistance and self-sabotage are common challenges that many people face when they try to achieve their goals or make positive changes in their lives. Resistance is the feeling of reluctance or avoidance that arises **when you are about to do something unfamiliar, uncomfortable or challenging.**

Self-sabotage is the intentional or unintentional action or inaction that undermines your progress and prevents you from accomplishing your goals.

Resistance and self-sabotage can have various causes, such as fear of failure, fear of success, fear of change, absence of comfort zone, low self-esteem, limiting beliefs, negative emotions, or past traumas. These can have various effects such as procrastination, perfectionism, distraction, avoidance, denial, rationalization or self-criticism.

To overcome resistance and self-sabotage, you need to identify and challenge the underlying causes and develop strategies to cope with them. Here are some remedial steps.

Acknowledge your resistance and self-sabotage

The first step is to become aware of your resistance and self-sabotage which affect your life. You can use tools such as journaling, meditation, or self-reflection to explore your thoughts and feelings and recognize your patterns and triggers. You can also use tools such as web searches, books, or podcasts to learn more about the causes and effects of resistance and self-sabotage (1,2&3).

Challenge your resistance and self-sabotage

The second step is to challenge your resistance and self-sabotage and change your mindset and behavior. You can use tools such as cognitive behavioral therapy, positive affirmations, or goal-setting to identify and reframe your negative thoughts, beliefs, and emotions, and replace them with more positive and empowering ones. You can also use tools such as action plans, rewards, or accountability partners to motivate and support yourself to take action toward your goals (1,4&5).

Practice self-compassion and gratitude

The third step is to practice self-compassion and gratitude and cultivate a positive and healthy relationship with your inner world. You can use tools such as mindfulness, meditation, or journaling to be kind and forgiving to yourself and acknowledge and appreciate your strengths and achievements. You can also use tools such as social support, hobbies, or self-care to nurture and nourish yourself.

By following these steps, you can overcome your resistance and self-sabotage, and create a more positive and empowering mindset.

References

1. https://psychologytoday.com
2. https://verywellmind.com
3. https://blog.calm.com
4. https://womenifesting.com
5. https://psychcentral.com

Books & Blogs

1: Self-Sabotaging: Why We Do It and How to Stop the Cycle - Verywell Mind

2: Self-Sabotage | Psychology Today

3: Self-Sabotaging: what it is, causes, and How to Stop — Calm Blog

4: How to Overcome Resistance FINALLY: Stop Sabotaging Yourself

5: Self-Sabotage: Why You Hold Yourself Back - Psych Central

6 Six Ways to Stop Sabotaging Yourself | Psychology Today

Mistakes We Make

Manifestation is the process of creating and attracting the reality that you desire by aligning your thoughts, emotions, and actions with the frequency of your desired outcomes. However, there are some common mistakes that people make while manifesting, which can hinder or delay their manifestation. But always remember that mistakes are only mistakes, not crimes. Here are some of them-

Being vague about your desires

If you are not clear and specific about what you want to manifest, you will not be able to send a coherent and powerful signal to the universe. You need to have a clear and detailed vision of your desired outcome (1&2).

Having a negative mindset

If you have negative thoughts, beliefs, and emotions, you will lower your vibration and attract more negativity. You need to have positive thoughts, beliefs, and emotions, and focus on the bright aspects of yourself, your life, and your reality. (1&2)

Focusing too much on current reality

If you focus too much on your current reality, especially the aspects that you don't like or want to change, you will reinforce them and create more resistance. You need to focus more on your desired reality and act as if it is already true and inevitable (1&2).

Being inconsistent with manifestation practice

If you are not consistent with your manifestation practice, such as visualization, affirmations, meditation, etc., you will not be able to maintain your alignment and attraction. You need to practice your manifestation techniques regularly and persistently and make them a part of your daily routine (1&2).

Doubting your ability to manifest your dreams

If you doubt your ability to manifest your dreams, you will create a self-fulfilling prophecy and thus sabotage your manifestation. You need to believe in your ability to manifest your dreams and trust the process and the timing of the universe (1&2).

Being impatient with your manifestation

If you are impatient with your manifestation, you will create anxiety and frustration, and interfere with the natural flow of manifestation. You need to be patient with your manifestation let go of the outcome and the timing, and trust that your desires are on their way to you (1&2).

Ignoring intuition and inner guidance

If you ignore your intuition and inner guidance, you will miss the signs, synchronicities, and feedback from the universe, and the opportunities and actions that are aligned with your manifestation. You need to listen to your intuition recognize the signals and inner guidance and follow them with faith and confidence (1&2).

Obsessing over the outcome

If you obsess over the outcome, you will create attachment and desperation, and repel your desires. You need to detach from the outcome and be open and flexible to the ways and forms that your desires may manifest (1&2).

Neglecting self-care

If you neglect self-care, you will lower your vibration and your well-being, and affect your manifestation. You need to take care of yourself and nurture and nourish your body, mind, and soul (1&2).

These are some of the common mistakes that people make while manifesting. By avoiding these mistakes, and following the tips and strategies mentioned above, you can improve your manifestation and create the desired outcome.

References-

1. https://gateofconsciousness.com
2. https://positiveaffirmationscenter.com

Books-

1: Avoid When Manifesting: 15 Common Mistakes to Watch Out For

2: The Top 9 Common Mistakes While Manifesting and How to Overcome Them

The law of attraction is the idea that you can attract what you want in life by aligning your thoughts, emotions, and actions with the frequency of your desired outcomes. Here are some books that can help you learn more about this topic and how to apply it to your life-

The Secret by Rhonda Byrne: This is one of the most popular and influential books on the law of attraction. It reveals the ancient wisdom and universal principles that can help you manifest anything you want, such as health, wealth, happiness, and love. It also features inspiring stories and testimonials from people who have used the law of attraction to achieve their dreams1.

Super Attractor by Gabrielle Bernstein: This book demystifies the concept of the law of attraction and manifestation by drawing on the author's life experiences. It teaches you how to co-create the life you want by aligning with the source of all creation and intelligence. It also offers practical tools and techniques to help you overcome your blocks, fears, and doubts, and become a super attractor2.

The Law of Attraction by Esther and Jerry Hicks: This book is based on the teachings of

Abraham, a group of non-physical entities channeled by Esther Hicks. It explains the basic principles and mechanics of the law of attraction, and how you can use it to joyously be, do, or have anything you desire. It also answers some of the most common questions and challenges that people have about the law of attraction3.

Feeling Good by Kenneth Wong: This book reveals the secret to manifesting, which is not about what you do, but how you feel. It shows you how to use your emotions as a guide and a magnet to attract what you want in life. It also provides practical exercises and tips to help you feel good, raise your vibration, and manifest your dream life4.

The Alchemist by Paulo Coelho: This is a classic and inspiring novel that tells the story of Santiago, a young shepherd who embarks on a journey to find his treasure and destiny. Along the way, he learns to listen to his heart, follow his dreams, and trust the signs and synchronicities of the universe. This book is a metaphor for the law of attraction and the power of your imagination5.

These are some of the best books on the law of attraction for beginners. I hope you enjoy reading them and applying them to your life.

Limiting beliefs are the negative thoughts that hold you back from achieving your goals and living your full potential. Negative patterns are the habitual behaviors that reinforce your limiting beliefs and prevent you from making positive changes. To overcome limiting beliefs and negative patterns, you need to

✓ **Identify and challenge them**

The first step is to become aware of your limiting beliefs and negative patterns, and how they affect your life. *Write down any negative thoughts and notice which ones come up repeatedly* – those are your limiting beliefs. Make a conscious effort to catch them, stop them, and replace them with more empowering thoughts

For example, if you think "I'm not good enough", you can replace it with "I have unique strengths and abilities".

✓ **Take action**

Taking action toward your goals can help build confidence and challenge limiting beliefs. *Break down your goals into small, achievable tasks and steps and take action towards them.* Celebrate your progress and achievements, and learn from your mistakes. **Surround yourself with positivity**: Surround yourself with people who believe in you and support your goals. Seek feedback and guidance from mentors, coaches, or friends who can help you grow and improve. **Avoid people who are negative, critical, or toxic, and who drain your energy and motivation.**

✓ **Develop your senses**

The better you get at using your senses, the better you'll be at using your imagination to positively shape the future. Think about best-case scenarios and visualize them in vivid and specific detail, as if they are already happening in the present moment. **Feel the positive emotions** that are associated with your desired outcomes, such as joy, gratitude, love, and excitement. **Act as if**

your desired outcomes are already true and inevitable, and take inspired and consistent actions that are aligned with them.

✓ **Get a cue**

Sometimes, we need space between ourselves and our triggers to bring ourselves back to the present, imagine our desired course of action, and choose a response that best supports it. A cue may be taking a deep breath or tapping your wrist three times. It could even be a phrase. When you're in the heat of, say, a conversation and feeling like you won't make it through, use your cue. This will activate your positive imagery and help you persevere.

By following these steps, you can overcome your limiting beliefs and negative patterns, and create a more positive and empowering mindset.

Intuition and creativity are two interrelated abilities that can help you access your inner wisdom and generate new ideas. **Intuition** is the ability to know or sense something without conscious reasoning, while **creativity** is the ability to produce something original and valuable. ***Both intuition and creativity can be developed with practice and training***. Here are some ways to do so-

☼ Meditate regularly

Meditation can help you quiet your mind, increase your awareness, and tune in to your intuition. Meditation can also stimulate your imagination, enhance your problem-solving skills, and foster your creative thinking. You can try different types of meditation, such as mindfulness, heartfulness, mantra, or guided meditation, and find what works best for you. Aim for at least 10 minutes of meditation per day (1&2).

✍ Keep a journal

Journaling can help you express your thoughts and feelings, clarify your goals and intentions, and discover your insights and inspirations. Journaling can also help you overcome your mental blocks, challenge your limiting beliefs, and unleash your creative potential. You can write freely, without censoring or judging yourself, and explore different topics, formats, and styles. You can also use journal prompts, such as questions, quotes, or images, to spark your intuition and creativity (3&4).

🏝 Engage in hobbies and activities that interest you

Hobbies and activities that interest you can help you relax, have fun, and stimulate your brain. Hobbies and activities that interest you can also help you develop new skills, explore new perspectives, and express your individuality. You can pursue hobbies and activities that are related to your goals or passions, or try something new and different. You can also combine or mix different hobbies and activities to create something unique and original (5).

🔔 Allow yourself to daydream and imagine

Daydreaming and imagining can help you access your subconscious mind, where your intuition and creativity reside. Daydreaming and imagining can also help you **visualize your desired outcomes, generate new possibilities, and expand your horizons.** You can daydream and imagine whenever you have some free time, such as before sleeping, after waking up, or during breaks. You can also use tools, such as **music, art, or stories, to enhance your daydreaming and imagining.**

Intuition and instinct are both forms of **inner guidance that can help us make decisions and navigate life situations.** However, they are not the same thing. Here are some key differences between intuition and instinct-

Intuition is voluntary and flexible, while instinct is automatic and fixed. Intuition operates with conscious awareness and choice, while instinct operates without conscious control or choice. Intuition can adapt and change according to the situation, while instinct is predictable and stable.

Intuition is based on subtle perception and knowing, while instinct is based on survival and adaptation. *Intuition relies on the subconscious mind, spiritual guidance, and collective consciousness, while instinct relies on the nervous system and genetic code.* Intuition helps us sense or know something beyond rational reasoning or analysis, while instinct helps us react for survival and reproductive success.

Intuition is influenced by emotions, beliefs, and spiritual guidance, while instinct is not influenced by emotions or beliefs. Intuition reflects our individuality and variability, while instinct reflects our commonality and universality. Intuition can be affected by our mood, mindset, and intuition, while instinct is unaffected by these factors.

To summarize, intuition and instinct are different ways of knowing and acting that serve different purposes. **Intuition is a voluntary, flexible, and subjective form of guidance** that helps us access our inner wisdom and creativity, while **instinct is an automatic, fixed, and objective form of guidance** that helps us ensure our survival and adaptation12.

Intuition and Fear This is a common question that many people struggle with. Intuition and fear are both forms of inner guidance that can help us make decisions and navigate life situations. However, they are not the same thing. Here are some key differences between intuition and fear-

Intuition is voluntary and flexible, while fear is automatic and fixed. Intuition operates with conscious awareness and choice, while fear operates without conscious control or choice. Intuition can adapt and change according to the situation, while fear is predictable and stable.

Intuition is based on subtle perception and knowing, while fear is based on survival and adaptation. Intuition relies on the subconscious mind, spiritual guidance, and collective consciousness, while fear relies on the nervous system and genetic code. Intuition helps us sense or know something beyond rational reasoning or analysis, while fear helps us react for survival and reproductive success.

Intuition is influenced by emotions, beliefs, and spiritual guidance, while fear is not influenced by emotions or beliefs. Intuition reflects our individuality and variability, while fear reflects our commonality and universality. Intuition can be affected by our mood, mindset, and intuition, while fear is unaffected by these factors.

To summarize, intuition and fear are different ways of knowing and acting that serve different purposes. Intuition is a voluntary, flexible, and subjective form of guidance that helps us access our inner wisdom and creativity, while fear is an automatic, fixed, and objective form of guidance that helps us ensure our survival and adaptation (1&2).

To distinguish between intuition and fear, you can also pay attention to how they feel in your body and mind. **Intuition often feels more like a pulling energy**, drawing you toward your best interests. **Fear often feels more like a pushing energy,** as if you want to avoid disappointment or ridicule. Intuition often feels calm and more certain, while fear often feels more anxious and doubtful. Intuition often feels more positive and empowering, while fear often feels more negative and limiting (3&4).

To trust your intuition and overcome your fear, you can also practice the following steps-

Meditate regularly

Meditation can help you quiet your mind, increase your awareness, and tune in to your intuition. Meditation can also help you reduce your stress, anxiety, and fear. You can try different types of meditation, such as mindfulness, mantra, or guided meditation, and find what works best for you. Aim for at least 10 minutes of meditation per day (5).

Keep a journal

Journaling can help you express your thoughts and feelings, clarify your goals and intentions, and discover your insights and inspirations. Journaling can also help you overcome your mental blocks, challenge your limiting beliefs, and unleash your creative potential. You can write freely, without censoring or judging yourself, and explore different topics, formats, and styles. You can also use journal prompts, such as questions, quotes, or images, to spark your intuition and creativity.

Ask for guidance

Asking for guidance can help you access your intuition and spiritual guidance. You can ask for guidance from your higher self, your spirit guides, your angels, or any other source that resonates with you. You can ask for guidance through prayer, affirmation, or intention, and then listen for the answers that come to you through your intuition, dreams, or synchronicities.

Take action

Taking action can help you test your intuition and overcome your fear. You can start by taking small, manageable steps that are aligned with your intuition and goals, and then observe the results and feedback that you get. You can also use your fear as a motivator and a challenge, rather than a deterrent and a barrier. **You can use the acronym F.E.A.R. to reframe your fear as Face it, explore it, Accept it, and Rise above it.**

By following these steps, you can distinguish between intuition and fear, and learn to trust your gut feeling.

3

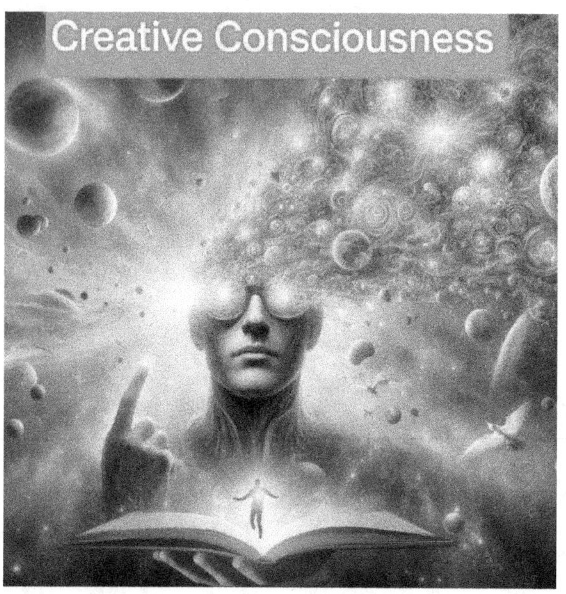

How to tap into the infinite intelligence and creative power of the universal mind

The universal mind is the source of all creation and intelligence in the universe. It is the infinite and eternal energy that pervades and sustains everything that exists. It is also the essence of who we are, as we are all expressions and extensions of the universal mind. By tapping into the infinite intelligence and creative power of the universal mind, we can access our true potential and manifest our dream life.

What is the universal mind?

The universal mind is the term used to describe the collective consciousness of all living beings, as well as the underlying intelligence and order of the physical world. The universal mind is also known by other names, such as the **quantum field, the source, the field of pure potentiality, the cosmic mind, the God mind, or simply God** (1,2&3).

The universal mind is not a personal or separate entity, but a universal and impersonal principle that operates through **natural laws and principles**. The universal mind is not a physical or material thing, but a metaphysical and spiritual reality that transcends time and space. The universal mind is not a static or fixed thing, but a dynamic and flexible thing that constantly evolves and expands.

The universal mind is the origin and destination of all creation and intelligence. It contains all the possibilities and potentials that ever were, are, or will be. It also contains all the knowledge and wisdom that ever were, are, or will be. **It is the ultimate source of inspiration, innovation, inventions and actions.**

Why tap into the universal mind?

Tapping into the universal mind can bring us many benefits, such as -

Enhanced intuition and insight

By tapping into the universal mind, we can access the infinite intelligence that guides and supports us every moment. We can receive new thoughts and ideas, bring forth inventions, make discoveries, and create new works of art (4).

Expanded awareness and perception

By tapping into the universal mind, **we can transcend the limitations of our ego and senses, and experience reality beyond appearances. We can see the interconnectedness and interdependence of all things and the underlying patterns and principles that govern the universe (5).**

Increased creativity and productivity

By tapping into the universal mind, we can unleash our creative potential and express our unique gifts and talents. We can also align our actions with the flow and rhythm of the universe, and achieve more with less effort and stress.

Improved health and well-being

By tapping into the universal mind, we can harmonize our body, mind, and soul, and activate our natural healing abilities. We can also balance our emotions and thoughts, and cultivate an optimistic attitude towards life.

Greater happiness and fulfillment

By tapping into the universal mind, we can connect with our true self and ultimate purpose, and live joyfully. We can also attract and manifest our desires, and enjoy the abundance and prosperity of the universe.

How to tap into the universal mind?

Tapping into the universal mind is not a complicated process, but a simple and natural one. It does not require any special skills or techniques, but only a sincere intention and a receptive attitude. Here are some ways to tap into the universal mind:

Meditate regularly

Meditation is one of the most effective ways to tap into the universal mind, as it helps us **quiet our minds, increase our awareness, and tune in to our intuition**. Meditation also helps us relax our body, calm our emotions, and clear our thoughts. By meditating regularly, we can create a direct and intimate connection with the universal mind, and receive its guidance and support.

Ask for guidance

Asking for guidance is another way to tap into the universal mind, as it shows our humility, curiosity, and openness. We can ask for guidance from the universal mind, our higher self, our spiritual guides, our angels, or any other source that resonates with us. We can ask for guidance through **prayer, affirmation, or intention,** and then listen for the answers that come to us through our **intuition, dreams, or synchronicities.**

Engage in creative activities

Engaging in creative activities is another way to tap into the universal mind, as it stimulates our **imagination, enhances our problem-solving skills, and fosters our creative thinking.** We can engage in creative activities that interest us, such as writing, painting, music, or gardening, and express our individuality and originality. By engaging in creative activities, we can access the infinite intelligence and creative power of the universal mind, and bring forth new creations.

Spend time with nature

Spending time with nature is another way to tap into the universal mind, as it helps us **reconnect** with the source of all life and intelligence. Nature is the manifestation and expression of the universal mind, and it reflects its beauty, harmony, and diversity. By spending time with nature, we can observe and appreciate the wonders and miracles of the universe, and feel its beauty, presence, and energy.

Practice gratitude and generosity

Practicing gratitude and generosity is another way to tap into the universal mind, as it helps us align with the frequency and vibration of the universe. **The universe is abundant and generous, and it responds to our gratitude and generosity.** By practicing gratitude and generosity, we can **acknowledge and appreciate** the gifts and blessings of the universe, and share them with others.

Conclusion

The universal mind is the source of all creation and intelligence in the universe, and it is also the essence of who we are. By tapping into the infinite intelligence and creative power of the universal mind, **we can access our true potential and manifest our dream life.** To tap into the universal mind, we can meditate regularly, ask for guidance, engage in creative activities, spend time in nature, and practice gratitude and generosity. By following these steps, we can create and attract the reality that we desire, and live our dream life.

References

1. https://deepakchopra.com
2. https://oursubconsciousmind.com
3. www.iitd.ac.in
4. www.zerotoinfintude.com
5. www.holistickingdom.com

4

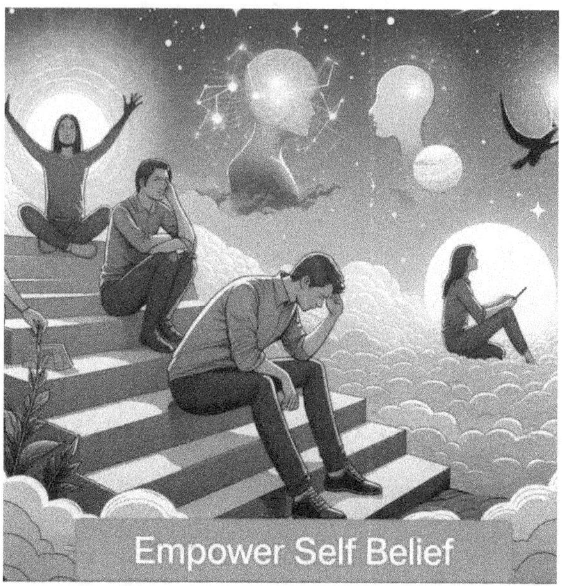

How to overcome limiting beliefs, fears, and negative patterns that block your manifestation abilities.

IN THE CASE OF HUMANS, THE FRUITS NEVER DEPEND ON THE ROOTS BUT ON HOW ONE MOOTS.

One of the biggest obstacles to manifest our dream life is **our mind**. Our mind can be best friend or worst enemy, depending on how we use it. *Our mind can create and attract the reality that we desire,* *deserve, reserve and conserve or it can block and repel.* The difference lies in our beliefs, fears, and patterns.

The universal mind serves what we desire, deserve, reserve and conserve.

Beliefs are the assumptions and convictions that **we hold about** ourselves and others. They shape our perception, interpretation, and expectation of reality.

Fears are the emotions and sensations that **we experience** when we face or anticipate a threat or danger. They trigger our **fight, flight or freeze response,** and affect our behavior and choices.

Patterns are the habitual and repetitive thoughts, feelings, and actions that **we engage in,** consciously or unconsciously. They form our personality, identity, and lifestyle.

Beliefs, fears, and patterns can be positive or negative, empowering or limiting, constructive or destructive.

- ✓ Positive, empowering, and constructive beliefs, fears, and patterns **can help us manifest our dream life**, as they align us with the frequency of our desired outcomes, and attract them from the quantum field and the universal mind.

- ✓ Negative, limiting, and destructive beliefs, fears, and patterns **can block our manifestation abilities,** as they misalign us with the frequency of our desired outcomes, and repel them from the quantum field and the universal mind.

Therefore, to overcome the blocks to our manifestation abilities, we need to *understand our limiting beliefs, fears, and negative patterns, and replace them with more positive, empowering, and constructive ones.*

Here are some steps we can take to do so

Identify our limiting beliefs, fears, and negative patterns

The first step is to identify the limiting beliefs, fears, and negative patterns, and how they affect life. We can use tools such as **journaling, meditation, or self-reflection to explore our thoughts and feelings and recognize the patterns and triggers.** We can also use tools such as web searches, books, or podcasts to learn more about the causes and effects of limiting beliefs, fears, and negative patterns (1,2&3).

Some examples of common limiting beliefs are-

I'm not good enough

I don't deserve it

It's too hard

It's too late

It's not possible

Some examples of common fears are-

Fear of failure

Fear of rejection

Fear of change

Fear of loss

Some examples of common negative patterns are-

Procrastination

Perfectionism

Self-criticism

Self-sabotage

Victim mentality

Challenge your limiting beliefs, fears, and negative patterns

The second step is to challenge the limiting beliefs, fears, and negative patterns, and change the mindset and behavior. We can use tools such as **cognitive behavioral therapy, positive affirmations, or goal-**

setting to identify and reframe negative thoughts, beliefs, and emotions, and replace them with more positive and empowering ones. We can also use tools such as action plans, rewards, or accountability partners to motivate and support ourselves to take action toward our ultimate goals (4,5&6).

Some examples of how to challenge and reframe the limiting beliefs -

I'm not good enough

I have unique strengths and abilities

I don't deserve it

I am worthy and deserve the best

It's too hard

I can overcome any challenge

It's too late

It's never too late to start

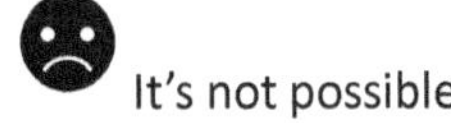 It's not possible

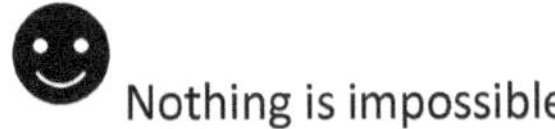 Nothing is impossible

Some examples of how to challenge and reframe our fears are:

Fear of failure

Failure is feedback, not final

Fear of what others will respond to

Your action and results will respond to

Fear of rejection

Rejection is redirection, not reflection

Fear of change

Change is an opportunity, not a threat

Fear of loss

☺ Loss is detachment, not deprivation

Some examples of how to challenge the negative patterns are-

☹ Procrastination

☺ do it now, not later

☹ Perfectionism

☺ Do your best, not the best

☹ Self-criticism

☺ Be kind, not harsh to yourself

☹ Self-sabotage

☺ Support yourself, never undermine

☹ Victim mentality

☺ Take responsibility, do not blame others

The third step is to **practice self-compassion and gratitude and cultivate a positive and healthy relationship with yourself**. You can use tools such as mindfulness, meditation, or journaling to be kind and forgiving to yourself and acknowledge and appreciate your strengths and achievements. You can also use tools such as social support, hobbies, or self-care to nurture and nourish yourself.

Some examples of how to practice self-compassion are-

😊 I will treat myself as I would treat a friend

😊 I will accept myself as I am, with all my flaws

😊 I will forgive myself for my mistakes, and learn from them

😊 I will speak to myself with love

😊 I will honour my feelings

Some examples of how to practice gratitude are-

😊 I will express my gratitude for the people, things, and experiences in my life

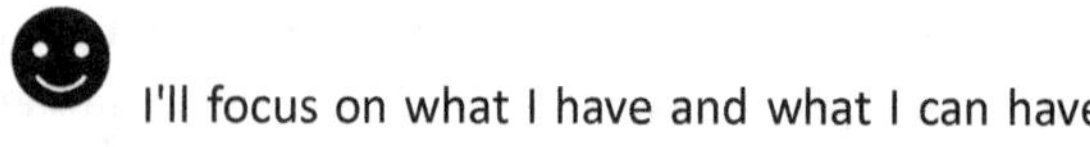 I'll focus on what I have and what I can have

 I will appreciate not only the big moments and achievements in life but also the small ones.

 I will celebrate my successes

I will be grateful for the present

Conclusion

Overcoming your limiting beliefs, fears, and negative patterns are key steps to manifest your dream life. By overcoming your blocks, you will align yourself with the frequency of your desired outcomes, and attract them from the quantum field and the universal mind. To overcome your blocks, you need to identify, challenge, and practice self-compassion and gratitude. By following these steps, you can overcome your limiting beliefs, fears, and negative patterns, and create and attract the reality that you desire.

References-

1. www.asana.com
2. www.hbr.org
3. www.visiting-subconscious.com
4. www.verywellmind.com
5. www.onebreathinstitute.com
6. www.tonyrobbins.com

Notes

Cognitive behavioral therapy (CBT) is a form of psychotherapy that helps you change your negative thoughts, beliefs, and emotions, and improve your mood and behavior. CBT can help you cope with various mental and physical health challenges, such as depression, anxiety, trauma, chronic pain, or stress (1&2).

To apply the principles of CBT to your daily life, you can follow these steps:

Identify your negative thoughts, beliefs, and emotions: The first step is to become aware of your negative thoughts, beliefs, and emotions, and how they affect your life. You can use tools such as journaling, meditation, or self-reflection to explore your thoughts and feelings and recognize your patterns and triggers. For example, you can write down what you think, feel, and do when you face a difficult situation, and how it impacts your well-being (3).

Challenge your negative thoughts, beliefs, and emotions: The second step is to challenge your negative thoughts, beliefs, and emotions, and replace them with more positive and realistic ones. You can use tools such as cognitive restructuring, positive affirmations, or goal-setting to identify and reframe your negative thoughts, beliefs, and emotions, and create more helpful and empowering ones. For example, you can question the validity and evidence of your negative thoughts, and find alternative ways of thinking that are more accurate and optimistic (4).

Practice positive thoughts, beliefs, and emotions: The third step is to practice your positive thoughts, beliefs, and emotions, and make them a part of your daily life. You can use tools such as visualization, gratitude, or mindfulness to reinforce your positive thoughts, beliefs, and emotions, and experience their benefits. For example, you can imagine yourself achieving your goals, express your appreciation for what you have, or focus on the present moment and your senses (5).

By following these steps, you can apply the principles of CBT to your daily life, and improve your mental and physical health. You can also seek professional help from a therapist who can guide you through the process of CBT, and provide you with feedback and support. CBT is a proven and effective therapy that can help you overcome your challenges and live a happier and healthier life.

References-

1: Cognitive Behavioral Therapy (CBT): What It Is & Techniques

2: Cognitive Behavioral Therapy for Depression: How Does It Work? - Healthline

3: How it works - Cognitive behavioral therapy (CBT) - NHS

4: How to Overcome Resistance FINALLY: Stop Sabotaging Yourself

5: 9 High Energy Strategies to Access Infinite Intelligence

CBT stands for cognitive behavioral therapy, which is a form of psychotherapy that helps you change your negative thoughts, beliefs, and emotions, and improve your mood and behavior (1). Here are some of the apps or websites that you can check out-

Moodfit-This is an app that helps you track your mood, thoughts, and activities, and provides you with personalized feedback and tips to improve your mental health. You can also access CBT worksheets, exercises, and audio guides to help you cope with various challenges, such as depression, anxiety, stress, or insomnia (2).

Woebot-This is an app that uses artificial intelligence to chat with you and provide you with CBT-based support and guidance. You can also learn CBT skills and techniques, such as cognitive restructuring, mindfulness, and gratitude, through interactive lessons and quizzes (3).

Think CBT-This is a website that provides free CBT worksheets, exercises, information handouts, self-help guides, audio therapy tools, and the Treatments That Work™ series. You can download and use these resources for various mental and physical health issues, such as panic, phobia, OCD, PTSD, insomnia, chronic pain, or eating disorders (4).

Therapist Aid-This is a website that provides free CBT worksheets, exercises, videos, and other tools for therapists and clients. You can find resources for various topics, such as cognitive distortions, core beliefs, the cognitive triangle, worry exploration, behavioral experiments, and more (5).

Psychology Tools- This is a website that provides free CBT worksheets, exercises, information handouts, audio therapy tools, and the Treatments That Work™ series. You can download and use these resources for various mental and physical health issues, such as depression, anxiety, trauma, chronic pain, or stress.

These are some of the apps or websites that offer free CBT resources. I hope you find them helpful and useful.

References -

1: Cognitive Behavioral Therapy (CBT): What It Is & Techniques

2: Moodfit - The #1 App for Your Mental Health

3: Woebot - Your charming robot friend who is ready to listen, 24/7

4: Free CBT Worksheets | Cognitive Behavioural Therapy Exercises | The Think CBT Workbook – www.psychologytools.com

5: CBT Worksheets | Therapist Aid: CBT Worksheets, Psychology Tools- www.psychwire.com

5

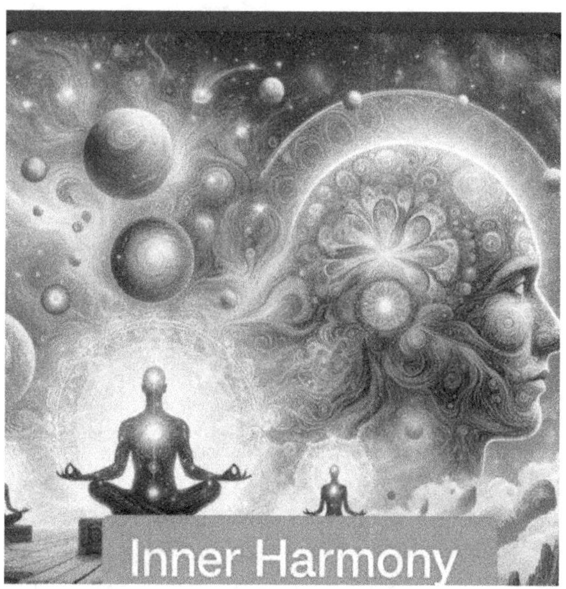

How to practice mindfulness, meditation, and visualization to enhance your connection with the universe and yourself.

The universe is the source of all creation and intelligence, and it is also the essence of who we are. We are all connected to the universe, and the universe is connected to us. By enhancing our connection with the universe and ourselves, we can access its infinite wisdom and creativity, and manifest our dream life.

One of the best ways to enhance our connection with the universe and ourselves is to practice mindfulness, meditation, and visualization. These are powerful tools that can help us cultivate awareness, focus, and intention, and align our thoughts, emotions, and actions with the frequency of our desired outcomes. In this chapter, we will explore how to practice mindfulness, meditation, and visualization, and how they can benefit us.

What is mindfulness?

Mindfulness is the practice **of paying attention to the present moment, with openness, curiosity, and acceptance. Mindfulness helps us become aware of our thoughts, feelings, sensations, and surroundings, without judging or reacting.** Mindfulness also helps us **become aware of our connection with the universe and ourselves, and appreciate the beauty and wonders of life (1&2).**

What is meditation?

Meditation is the practice of training our minds to achieve a state of calmness, clarity,

and concentration. Meditation helps us to keep calm our minds, reduce our stress, and enhance our well-being. Meditation also helps us to tap into the infinite intelligence and creative power of the universe and ourselves, and receive its guidance and support (3).

What is visualization?

Visualization is the practice of using our imagination to create mental images of what we want to manifest, and how we want to feel. Visualization helps us activate our subconscious mind, which is the bridge between the physical and the metaphysical realms. Visualization also helps us attract our desired outcomes from the quantum field and the universal mind and allows us to manifest our physical reality.

How to practice mindfulness, meditation, and visualization?

To practice mindfulness, meditation, and visualization, we need to set aside some time, and space and follow some basic steps. Here choose a comfortable posture- You can sit, stand, lie down, or walk, as long as you can keep your spine straight and your body relaxed. You can also use a cushion, a chair, a mat, or any other support that suits you.

Choose a suitable time

You can practice at any time of the day, but preferably when you are not too tired or too busy. You can also choose a time that matches your intention, such as morning for setting your goals, evening for reflecting on your day, or night for relaxing and sleeping.

Choose a quiet place

You can practice in any place that is free from distractions and noises, such as your bedroom, your living room, your garden, or a park. You can also use headphones, music, or sounds to create a peaceful and pleasant atmosphere.

Set an intention

Before you start, you can set an intention for your practice, such as what you want to achieve, how you want to feel, or what you want to manifest. You can also use a mantra, a word, or a phrase that resonates with you, such as "I am calm", "I am grateful", or "I am abundant".

Breathe deeply

You can start by taking a few deep breaths, and focus on your inhalation and exhalation. You can also use a breathing technique, such as counting your breaths, or following a pattern, such as 4-7-8 (inhale for 4 seconds, hold for 7 seconds, exhale for 8 seconds).

Practice mindfulness

You can practice mindfulness by observing your thoughts, feelings, sensations, and surroundings, **without judging and reacting**. You can also practice mindfulness by focusing on one thing at a time, such as your breath, your body, your senses, or an object. You can also practice mindfulness by being fully present and engaged in whatever you are doing, such as eating, walking, or listening.

Practice meditation

You can practice meditation by training your mind to **achieve a state of calmness, clarity, and concentration**. You can also practice meditation by using a technique, such as mindfulness meditation, heartfulness meditation, transcendental meditation, or guided meditation. You can also practice meditation by following a teacher, a video, or an app, such as Moodfit, Woebot, or Think CBT.

Practice visualization

You can practice visualization by using your imagination to create mental images of what you want to manifest, and how you want to feel. You can also practice visualization by using a technique, such as creative visualization, guided imagery, or a vision board. You can also practice visualization by following a script, a video, or an app, such as Visualization Meditation: 8 exercises to add to your practice, How to Practice Visualization Meditation: 3 Best Scripts, or Feeling Isolated? Try This 20-Minute Connection Practice.

How to benefit from mindfulness, meditation, and visualization?

To benefit from mindfulness, meditation, and visualization, we need to practice them regularly and consistently and apply them to our daily life. Here are some tips-

Practice daily

You can practice mindfulness, meditation, and visualization every day, for a few minutes, and gradually increase the duration and frequency of your practice. You can also practice at different times of the day, depending on your needs and preferences.

Practice with others

You can practice mindfulness, meditation, and visualization with others, such as your family, friends, or a group, and share your experiences and insights. You can also practice with a teacher, a coach, or a therapist, who can guide you and support you.

Practice with Variety

You can practice mindfulness, meditation, and visualization with variety, try different techniques, methods, and tools, and see what works best for you. You can also practice with different intentions, goals, and outcomes, and see what you can manifest.

Practice with joy

You can practice mindfulness, meditation, and visualization with joy, and enjoy the process and the results. You can also practice with gratitude and appreciate the gifts and blessings of the universe.

Conclusion

Mindfulness, meditation, and visualization are powerful tools that can help us enhance our connection with the universe and ourselves, and manifest our dream life. By practicing mindfulness, meditation, and visualization, we can cultivate awareness, focus, and intention, and align our thoughts, emotions, and actions with the frequency of our desired outcomes. By following the steps and tips mentioned above, we can practice mindfulness, meditation, and visualization, and benefit from them.

References

1. www.blog.calm.com
2. www.positivesychology.com
3. www.mindful.org

6

How to apply the law of attraction, the law of vibration, and other universal laws to attract what you want in life.

The universe is governed by natural laws and principles that operate at every level of existence, from the physical to the metaphysical world. These laws and principles are the keys to understand and influence the reality that we experience, and we desire. By applying these laws and principles in our life, we can align ourselves with the frequency and vibration of our desired outcomes, and thus attract them from the quantum field and the universal mind.

One of the most well-known and widely used laws and principles is the **law of attraction**, which states that **like attracts like**, and **we attract what we think, feel, and do. Superposition, which allows particles to exist in multiple states until measured and observed, echoes the idea that reality is not fixed and that consciousness can affect outcomes—an idea that aligns with the law of attraction's emphasis on the power of thought to influence reality.**

However, the law of attraction is not the only law or principle that affects our manifestation abilities. Some other laws and principles complement and support the law of attraction, and that we need to be aware of and apply in our life. Some of these laws and principles are-

The law of vibration

This law states that **everything in the universe is energy and vibration and has a specific frequency and wavelength**. This law also states **that we can change our vibration and frequency by changing our thoughts, emotions, and actions and thus we can match our vibration and frequency with the vibration and frequency of our desired outcomes.**

Entanglement where particles remain connected across vast distances, reflects the interconnectedness of all things, a key principle to Sankhya Yoga's understanding of the universe. It also resonates with the law of vibration, which suggests that everything is connected through vibrational energy.

Interference patterns demonstrate how waves can constructively or destructively combine, which can further be seen as a metaphor for how positive and negative thoughts (vibrations) might interact through the law of attraction, influencing the manifestation of one's reality.

The law of correspondence

This law states that as within, so is outer, and that our **outer world is a reflection of our inner world.** This law also states that we can change our outer world by changing our inner world and that we can create harmony and congruence between our inner and outer worlds.

The law of action

This law states that **action is required** to manifest our desires and that we need to take inspired and aligned action towards our goals. This law also states that we need to act as if our desires have already come true and are inevitable and that we need to follow our intuition and inner guidance.

The law of cause and effect

This law states that **for every effect, there is a cause, and for every cause, there is an effect** and <u>we are responsible for the causes and effects that we face.</u> This law also states that we can create positive and empowering causes and effects by choosing positive and empowering thoughts, emotions, and actions.

The law of polarity

This law states that **everything has an opposite** also and everything exists on a continuum. <u>**We can shift from one pole to another by changing our perspective and attitude.**</u> This law also states that we can use the challenges, we face as opportunities and catalysts for growth and transformation.

These are some of the laws and principles that can help us apply the law of attraction and manifest our dream life. By understanding and applying these laws and principles, we can create and attract the reality that we desire and can live our dream life.

How to apply the law of attraction, the law of vibration, and other universal laws?

To apply the law of attraction, the law of vibration, and other universal laws, we need to follow some basic steps. Here are some suggestions-

✓ **Set your intention**

Before you start, you need to set your intention for **what you want to manifest, and why you want to manifest it.** You need to have a clear and specific vision of your desired outcomes and strong and positive reasons to justify it. You can also use a mantra, a word, or a phrase that resonates with you, such as "I am healthy", "I am wealthy", or "I am happy".

✓ **Raise your vibration**

You need to raise your vibration and frequency **to match** the vibration and frequency of your desired outcomes. You can do this by changing your thoughts, emotions, and actions, and **choosing positive and empowering ones.** You can also use tools such as meditation, gratitude, or music to raise your vibration and frequency.

✓ **Take action**

You need to take action toward your goals and act as if your desires have already come true and inevitable. You can do this by **following your intuition and inner guidance,**

and taking inspired and aligned action. You can also use tools such as goal-setting, planning, or feedback to take action and measure your progress.

✓ Trust the process

You need to trust the process and the timing of the universe and **let go of the outcome and the procedure.** You can do this by **detaching from the outcome** and being open and flexible to the ways and forms that your desires may manifest. You can also use tools such as affirmations, visualization, or surrender to trust the process and the time taken by the universe.

✓ Receive and appreciate

You need to receive and appreciate your manifestations and acknowledge and celebrate your successes. You can do this by **expressing your gratitude for the gifts and blessings of the universe and sharing them with others**. You can also use tools such as journaling, reflection, or celebrations to receive and appreciate your manifestations.

How to benefit from the law of attraction, the law of vibration, and other universal laws?

To benefit from the law of attraction, the law of vibration, and other universal laws, we need to practice them **regularly and consistently and apply them to our day-to-day life.** Here are some tips-

✓ **Practice daily**

You can practice the law of attraction, the law of vibration, and other universal laws every day, for a few minutes, and gradually increase the duration and frequency of your practice. You can also practice at different times of the day, depending on your needs and preferences.

✓ **Practice with others**

You can practice the law of attraction, the law of vibration, and other universal laws with others, such as your family, friends, or a group, and share your experiences and insights. You can also practice with a teacher, a coach, or a mentor, who can guide you and support you.

✓ Practice with variety

You can practice the law of attraction, the law of vibration, and other universal laws with variety, and try different techniques, methods, and tools, and see what works best for you. You can also practice with different intentions, goals, and outcomes, and see what you can manifest.

✓ Practice with joy

You can practice the law of attraction, the law of vibration, and other universal laws with joy, and enjoy the process and the results. You can also practice with gratitude and appreciate the gifts and blessings of the universe.

Conclusion

The law of attraction, the law of vibration, and other universal laws are the keys to understand and influence the reality that we experience and desire. By applying these laws and principles to our life, we can align ourselves with the frequency and vibration of our desired outcomes, and attract them from the quantum field and the universal mind. By following the steps and tips mentioned above, we can apply the law of attraction, the law of vibration, and other universal laws, and benefit from them.

References Blogs-

The Law of Vibration: How to Use it to Manifest Your Desires - Mindvalley Blog

The Law of Vibration Explained in 3 Simple Steps - The Law of Attraction

The Law of Correspondence: How to Use it to Manifest Your Desires - Mindvalley Blog

The Law of Correspondence: How to Use it to Manifest Your Desires - The Law of Attraction

The Law of Action: How to Use it to Manifest Your Desires - Mindvalley Blog

The Law of Action: How to Use it to Manifest Your Desires - The Law of Attraction

The Law of Cause and Effect: How to Use it to Manifest Your Desires - Mindvalley Blog

The Law of Cause and Effect: How to Use it to Manifest Your Desires - The Law of Attraction

The Law of Polarity: How to Use it to Manifest Your Desires - Mindvalley Blog

The Law of Polarity: How to Use it to Manifest Your Desires - The Law of Attraction

The Secret by Rhonda Byrne

The Power of Your Subconscious Mind by Joseph Murphy

The Universal Mind: There is But One Consciousness by Peter Weisz

The Universal Mind: The Evolution of Machine Intelligence and Human Psychology by Xiphias Press

The Universal Mind: The Seven States of Consciousness by Michael Goddart

The Law of Attraction the Basics of the Teachings of Abraham] by Esther and Jerry Hicks

The Law of Attraction: How to Make It Work for You by Jack Canfield

The Law of Attraction: How to Use the Law of Attraction to Manifest Positive Energy, Better Relationships, More Money and Success by Jenny Hashkins

7

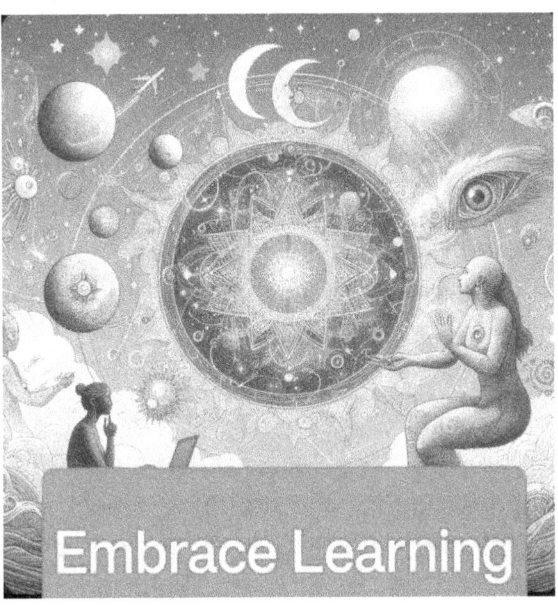

How to use gratitude, affirmations, and intention to amplify your manifestation power.

Manifestation is the process of bringing thoughts and desires into reality through focused intention and positive energy. Whether it be attracting abundance, fostering better relationships, or achieving personal goals, manifestation techniques aim to align our thoughts and emotions with the reality we wish to create.

One of the most effective and simple way to amplify our manifestation power is to use gratitude, affirmation, and intention. These are powerful tools that can help us cultivate a positive and abundant mindset, and attract more of what we want in our lives. In this chapter, we will explore how to use gratitude, affirmation, and intention, and how these can benefit us.

What is gratitude?

Gratitude is the feeling and expression of **appreciation for the present moment and the blessings in our lives.** Gratitude helps us shift our focus from lack to abundance, and recognize the opportunities and possibilities that surround us. Gratitude also helps us align our energy with the frequency of abundance, and attract more of what we desire into our lives (1&2).

"I am deeply thankful for the unwavering support and kindness that has been bestowed upon me. Your generosity has

illuminated my path and enriched my journey beyond measure."

What is affirmation?

Affirmation is the statement and repetition of positive and empowering words or phrases that reflect our desired outcomes. Affirmation **helps us reprogram our subconscious mind, and replace our negative and limiting beliefs with positive and empowering ones.** Affirmation also helps us to activate our subconscious mind, which is the bridge between the physical and the metaphysical realms (3&4).

"With every breathe I take; I affirm the strength within me. I am capable, resilient, and full of potential. I embrace the journey ahead, confident in my ability to rise above challenges and achieve greatness."

What is intention?

Intention is the clear and specific vision and purpose of **what we want to manifest, and why we want to manifest it.** Intention helps us to focus our attention and energy on our desired outcomes, and create a strong and positive emotional connection with them. Intention also helps us communicate our desires to the universe, and invite its support and guidance.

"I set forth with a clear vision and a determined heart. My intentions are anchored in purpose, guiding my actions towards meaningful achievements and positive impact."

How to use gratitude, affirmation, and intention?

To use gratitude, affirmation, and intention, we need to **set aside some time and space and follow some basic steps**. Here are some suggestions-

Choose a comfortable posture

You can sit, stand, lie down, or walk, as long as you can keep your spine straight and your body relaxed. You can also use a cushion, a chair, a mat, or any other support that suits you.

Choose a suitable time

You can use gratitude, affirmation, and intention at any time of the day, but preferably when you are not too tired or too busy. You can also choose a time that matches your intention, such as morning for setting your goals, evening for reflecting on your day, or night for relaxing and sleeping.

Choose a quiet place

You can use gratitude, affirmation, and intention in any place that is free from distractions and noises, such as your bedroom, your living room, your garden, or a park. You can also use headphones, music, or sounds to create a peaceful and pleasant atmosphere.

Express gratitude

Start by expressing gratitude for the present moment and the blessings in your life. You can use tools such as journaling, meditation, or prayer to express your gratitude. You can also use tools such as gratitude lists, gratitude jars, or gratitude letters to express your gratitude. For example, **you can write** down or say out loud three things that you are grateful for today, and how they make you feel.

State your affirmations

With sincerity and confidence, state your affirmations that reflect your desired outcomes. You can use tools **such** as writing, speaking, or recording to state your affirmations. You can also use tools such as affirmation cards, affirmation posters, or affirmation apps to state your affirmations. For example, you can write down or say out loud positive and empowering statements, such as "I am healthy", "I am wealthy", or "I am happy".

Set your intention

With clarity and specificity, set your intention for what you want to manifest, and why you want to manifest it. You can use tools such as visualization, meditation, or scripting to set your intention. You can also use tools such as intention cards, intention bracelets, or intention Diyas (candles) to set your intention. For example, you can imagine or write down what you want to manifest, such as a new job, a new relationship, or a new house, and how it will make you feel, such as fulfilled, loved, or comfortable.

Repeat daily

Consistency is key. Make it a daily practice, ideally at the same time each day, to use gratitude, affirmation, and intention. You can also use tools such as reminders, alarms, or calendars to track your practice.

How to benefit from gratitude, affirmation, and intention?

To benefit from gratitude, affirmation, and intention, we need to practice regularly and consistently and apply them to our daily life. Here are some tips-

Practice daily

You can practice gratitude, affirmation, and intention every day, even for a few minutes, and gradually increase the duration and frequency of your practice. You can also practice at different times of the day, depending on your needs and preferences.

Practice with others

You can practice gratitude, affirmation, and intention with others, such as your family, friends, or a group, and share your experiences and insights. You can also practice with a teacher, a coach, or a mentor, who can guide you and support you.

Practice with Variety

You can practice gratitude, affirmation, and intention with variety, try different tools, methods, and formats, and see what works best for you. You can also practice with different intentions, goals, and outcomes, and see what you can manifest.

Practice with joy

You can practice gratitude, affirmation, and intention with joy and enjoy the process and the results. You can also practice with gratitude and appreciate the gifts and blessings of the universe and yourself.

Conclusion

Gratitude, affirmation, and intention are powerful tools that can help us to amplify our manifestation power, and attract more of what we want in our life. By using gratitude, affirmation, and intention, we can cultivate a positive and abundant mindset, and align our energy with the frequency of our desired outcomes. By following the steps and tips mentioned above, we can use gratitude, affirmation, and intention, and benefit from these.

References

1. www.blog.gratefulness.me
2. www.medium.com
3. www.mindlake.co.uk
4. www.fastercapital.com

8

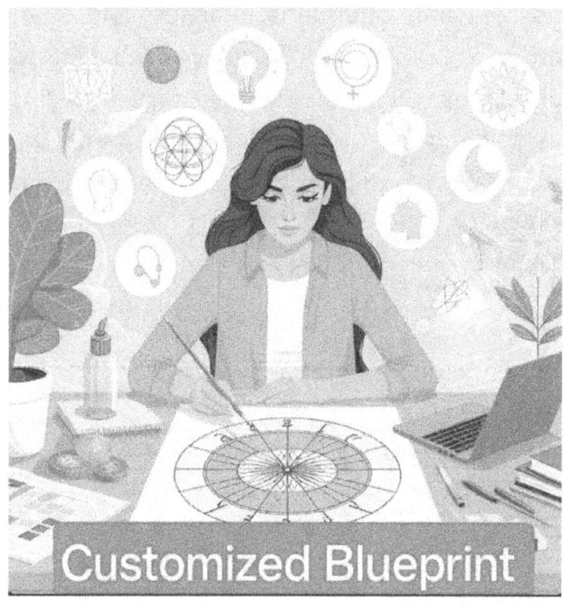

How to create a personalized manifestation plan that suits your goals, personality, and lifestyle

Manifestation is the process of turning your thoughts and desires into reality through the power of your mind and the law of attraction. However, manifestation is **not a one-size-fits-all technique** that works the same way for everyone. Each person has different goals, personality, and lifestyle, and therefore needs a different approach for manifestation.

A personalized manifestation plan is a customized and tailored plan that suits individual needs and preferences and helps one to achieve his specific goals. A personalized manifestation plan can help to overcome your challenges, optimize your strengths, and maximize results. A personalized manifestation plan can also help to enjoy the process and the journey of manifestation, and thus make it more rewarding.

In this chapter, we will explore how to create a personalized manifestation plan that suits our goals, personality, and lifestyle. We will cover the following steps-

Defining goals

The first step is to define your goals and what you want to manifest. You need to have a clear and specific vision of your desired outcomes and a strong and positive reason for wanting them. You can use tools such as journaling, visualization, or scripting to define your goals and what you want to manifest (1).

Assess your personality

The second step is to assess your personality and what makes you unique. You need to know your strengths and weaknesses, your likes and dislikes, your values and beliefs, and your habits and patterns. You can use tools such as personality tests, self-reflection, or feedback to assess your personality and what makes you unique (2&3). (SWOT analysis)

Evaluate your lifestyle

The third step is to evaluate your lifestyle and what influences your daily life. You need to consider your environment, your relationships, your health, your finances, and your time. You can use tools such as lifestyle audits, surveys, or trackers to evaluate your lifestyle and what influences your daily life (5).

Choose your methods

The fourth step is to choose your methods and what works best for you. You need to select the techniques, tools, and resources that resonate with you, and that are compatible with your goals, personality, and lifestyle. You can use tools such as web search, books, or podcasts to choose your methods that works best for you.

Create your plan

The fifth step is to create your plan and how you will implement it. You need to organize your methods into a structured manner and prepare a manageable plan. Also set a timeline and milestones for your progress and results. You can use tools such as diary-planners, calendars, or apps to create your plan and how you will implement it.

Execute your plan

The sixth step is to execute your plan and take action toward your goals. You need to follow your plan with consistency, commitment and adjustment as and when needed. You can use tools such as reminders, rewards, or accountability partners to execute your plan and take action towards your goals.

How to benefit from a personalized manifestation plan?

To benefit from a personalized manifestation plan, you need to practice it regularly and consistently and apply it to your daily life. Here are some tips-

Practice daily

You can practice your personalized manifestation plan every day, even for a few minutes, and gradually increase the duration and frequency of your practice. You can also practice at different times of the day, depending on your needs and preferences.

Practice with others

You can practice your personalized manifestation plan with others, such as your family, friends, or a group, and share your experiences and insights. You can also practice with a teacher, a coach, or a mentor, who can guide you and support you.

Practice with Variety

You can practice your personalized manifestation plan with variety, try different methods, tools, and resources, and see what works best for you. You can also practice with different goals, outcomes, and scenarios, and see what you can manifest.

Practice with joy

You can practice your personalized manifestation plan with joy, and enjoy the process and the results. You can also practice with gratitude and appreciate the gifts and blessings of the universe.

Conclusion

A personalized manifestation plan is a customized and tailored plan that suits your goals, personality, and lifestyle, and helps you achieve your specific goals. By creating and practicing a personalized manifestation plan, you can overcome your challenges, optimize your strengths, and maximize your results. You can also enjoy the process and the journey of manifestation, and make it more rewarding.

References-

1. www.101planners.com
2. www.aglowlifestyle.com
3. www.blog.mindvalley.com

4.   www.thelawofattraction.com

Some common mistakes people make when creating a personalized plan are-

Not defining their goals clearly and specifically, and not having a strong and positive reason for wanting them. This can lead to confusion, lack of motivation, and poor results.

Not assessing their personality and lifestyle, and not choosing methods and tools that suit their needs and preferences. This can lead to frustration, boredom, and inefficiency.

Not creating a structured and manageable plan, and not setting a timeline and milestones for their progress and results. This can lead to procrastination, distraction, and inconsistency.

Not following the plan with consistency and commitment, and not adjusting it as needed. This can lead to stagnation, resistance, and failure.

Not enjoying the process and the results, and not expressing gratitude for the gifts and blessings of the universe and themselves. This can lead to dissatisfaction, negativity, and loss of manifestation power.

To avoid these mistakes, you can follow the steps and tips mentioned in the previous chapter, and create a personalized manifestation plan that suits your goals, personality and lifestyle.

You can use manifestation to improve your career by following these steps-

Define your career goals and also what you want to achieve. Be clear and specific about your desired outcomes and have a strong and positive reason for wanting it.

Raise your vibration and frequency to match the vibration and frequency of your desired outcomes. You can do this by changing your thoughts, emotions, and actions with positivity. You can also use tools such as meditation, gratitude, or music to raise your vibration and frequency (1&2).

Take action towards your goals, and act as if your desires are already true and inevitable. You can do this by following your intuition and inner guidance, and taking inspired and aligned action. You can also use tools such as goal-setting, planning, or feedback to take action and measure your progress (3&4).

Trust the process and the timing of the universe, and let go the outcome. You can do this by detaching from the outcome and being open and flexible to the ways and forms that your desires may manifest. You can also use tools such as affirmations, visualization, or surrender to trust the process and the timing of the universe (5).

Receive and appreciate your manifestations, and acknowledge and celebrate your successes. You can do this by expressing your gratitude for the gifts and blessings of the universe and sharing them with others. You can also use tools such as journaling, reflection, or celebration to receive and appreciate your manifestations.

By following these steps, you can use manifestation to improve your career and attract more opportunities, growth, and satisfaction.

References

1. www.careercontessa.com
2. www.hive.com
3. www.selfmadeladies.com
4. www.blog.amphy.com
5. www.wikihow.com

9

How to recognize and interpret the signals, synchronicities, and feedback from the universe

The universe is constantly communicating with us, sending us signals, synchronicities, and feedback that guide us and help us to manifest our desires. However, sometimes we may miss or ignore these messages, or misunderstand their meaning. How can we become more aware and receptive of the universe's communication, and learn to interpret it correctly?

In this chapter, we will **explore how to recognize and interpret the signals, synchronicities, and feedback from the universe, and how they can benefit us.**

What are signals, synchronicities, and feedback from the universe?

Signals, synchronicities, and feedback from the universe are different ways in which the universe speaks to us, using **the language of symbols, metaphors, and coincidences.** Here are some definitions and examples-

Signals/signs are events, objects, or phenomena that appear in our reality and have a symbolic or metaphorical meaning. They are often related to our thoughts, feelings, or intentions, and serve as confirmation, guidance, or warning. For example, seeing a rainbow after a storm may be a sign of hope and renewal, seeing a feather on the ground may be a sign of angelic presence, or seeing a red light may be a sign to stop and reconsider (1&2).

Synchronicities are **meaningful coincidences** that occur when two or more seemingly unrelated events happen at the same time or in a sequence and have a connection or significance for us. They are often related to our questions, desires, or goals, and serve as answers, opportunities, or manifestations. For example, seeing the same number repeatedly may be a synchronicity that carries a message or a code, meeting someone who shares your interest or passion may be a synchronicity that leads to a collaboration or a relationship, or finding a book that you have been looking for maybe a synchronicity that provides you the information or inspiration you need (3 &4).

Feedback is the response or reaction that we receive from the universe as a result of our actions, choices, or behaviors. It is often related to our lessons, challenges, or growth, and serves as evaluation, correction, or encouragement. For example, receiving a compliment or a reward may be feedback that indicates that we are doing well and on the right track, receiving a criticism or a setback may be feedback that indicates that we need to improve or change something, or receiving a surprise or a gift may be feedback that indicates that we are appreciated and supported.

How to recognize signals, synchronicities, and feedback from the universe?

To recognize signs, synchronicities, and feedback from the universe, we need to be **more aware and attentive** of what is happening around us and within us. We need to **pay attention to the details, patterns, and feelings** that may otherwise escape our notice. Here are some tips to help us recognize signals, synchronicities, and feedback from the universe-

Practice mindfulness

Mindfulness is the practice of **paying attention to the present moment, with openness, curiosity, and acceptance.** Mindfulness helps us to become more aware of our thoughts, feelings, sensations, and surroundings, without judging or reacting. Mindfulness also helps us to become more aware of our connection with the universe and appreciate the beauty and wonders of life.

Ask for guidance

Asking for guidance is the practice of expressing our questions, desires, or intentions to the universe, and inviting its support and assistance. Asking for guidance helps us **clarify our goals and challenges, and align our energy and vibration with our desired outcomes.** Asking for guidance also helps us to open our mind and heart to receive the signals, synchronicities, and feedback that the universe may send us.

Trust your intuition

Trusting to intuition is the practice of listening to and following your inner voice, wisdom, and guidance. Trusting to intuition helps us discern the meaning and significance of the signals, synchronicities, and feedback that we encounter, and to act on accordingly. Trusting to intuition also helps us to **tune with the frequency and communication with the universe to co-create the reality that we want.**

How to interpret signals, synchronicities, and feedback from the universe?

To interpret signals, synchronicities, and feedback from the universe, we need to **use our intuition, logic, and common sense.** We need to **consider the context, the timing, and the relevance of the signals, synchronicities, and feedback that we receive, and how these relate to our situation and goals.** Here are some tips to help us interpret signals, synchronicities, and feedback from the universe-

🧠 Look the patterns and meanings

Looking at the patterns of the events and understanding their meaning is the process of **finding the connections and significance of the signals, synchronicities, and feedback that we receive.** It also helps us understand the message and the purpose of the universe's communication, and the way it works in our life. Further it helps us to recognize the themes and lessons that the universe wishes for us to learn and master.

Use resources and references

Using resources and references is the **process of consulting the sources and tools that can help us to interpret the signals, synchronicities, and feedback that we receive.** It also helps us to gain more insight and perspective on the universe's communication, and validate our intuition and logic. Further it helps us to learn more about the symbols, metaphors, and codes that the universe uses to communicate with us.

Take action and experiment

Taking action and experimenting is the process of applying and testing the signals, synchronicities, and feedback that we receive. It also **helps us to confirm and manifest** the universe's communication, and see the results and consequences of our choices and behaviors. Further it **helps us to adjust and improve our manifestation plan, and receive more signals, synchronicities, and feedback from the universe.**

How to benefit from signals, synchronicities, and feedback from the universe?

To benefit from signals, synchronicities, and feedback from the universe, we need to practice regularly, consistently and apply them to our daily life. Here are some tips to help us benefit from signals, synchronicities, and feedback from the universe-

Practice gratitude

Practicing gratitude is to express appreciation for the signals, synchronicities, and feedback that we receive from the universe and acknowledge their value and its impact on our life. It also helps us to **attract more signals, synchronicities, and feedback from the universe, and thus increases our vibration and frequency.** Further it helps us to **cultivate a positive and perfect mindset to** enjoy the process and the journey of manifestation.

Share the experiences

Sharing the experiences is the practice of communicating your signals, synchronicities, and feedback **with others, and to learn from their experiences.** It also helps us to inspire and support others, and create a community and a network of like-minded people. Further it helps us to gain more feedback and validation to expand our knowledge and awareness.

Have fun

The practice of enjoying and celebrating the signals, synchronicities, and feedback that we receive from the universe and seeing them as a form of communication and interaction with the universe, have a lot of fun. It also helps us to **relax, let go of our worries and doubts and trust the universe and its timing.** Further it helps us to appreciate the creativity of the universe and co-create the reality that we realised.

Conclusion

Signals, synchronicities, and feedback from the universe are different ways that the universe speaks to us, using the language of symbols, metaphors, and coincidences. By recognizing and interpreting them, we can receive the guidance and support that is needed to manifest our desires. By following the tips mentioned above, we can benefit from the signals, synchronicities and feedback from the universe and can live a more magical and meaningful life.

References

1. www.throughthephases.com
2. www.blog.mindvalley.com
3. www.thelawofattraction.com
4. www.yourtango.com

10

How to celebrate your success, learn from your failures, and enjoy the journey of manifesting your dream life

We all have goals and dreams that we want to achieve in life. It may be starting a business, travelling the world, finding love, or making a difference, we are constantly striving for the desired outcome. But along the way, we may encounter obstacles, challenges, and setbacks that can make us doubtful and affect our abilities. **How do we overcome these difficulties and keep on moving forward?** How do we celebrate our success and learn from our failures? And most importantly, how do we enjoy the journey of manifesting our dream life?

In this chapter, we will explore some strategies and tips that can help you to do just that. We will discuss how to:

> - **Adopt a growth mindset that embraces challenges and feedback**
> - **Celebrate your success, both big and small, in healthy and meaningful ways**
> - **Learn from your failures and use them as opportunities for improvement**
> - **Enjoy the journey of manifesting your dream life by being grateful, optimistic and aware**

Adopt a Growth Mindset

One of the key factors that determines how we respond to success and failure is our mindset. According to psychologist Carol

Dweck, there are two types of mindsets: fixed and growth1. A fixed mindset is the belief that our abilities and talents are fixed and cannot be changed. A growth mindset is the belief that our abilities and talents can be developed and improved through effort and learning.

People with **a fixed mindset** tend to avoid challenges, give up easily, ignore feedback, and feel threatened by the success of others. They believe that **success is a result of innate talent and that failure is a sign of inadequacy**. They often have a **fear of failure and a need for validation.** They may also tend to compare themselves to others and **feel insecure or jealous.**

People with a **growth mindset** tend to embrace challenges, persist in the face of obstacles, seek feedback, and learn from the success of others. They believe that **success is a result of hard work and that failure is a source of learning.** They have a curiosity and a passion for learning and improvement. They may also tend to **focus on their progress and goals and feel confident and inspired**.

As you can see, a growth mindset can help you cope with success and failure more positively. It can also help you enjoy the journey of manifesting your dream life, as you will see every experience as an opportunity to grow and learn. To adopt a growth mindset, you can-

- 👍 Challenge yourself to try new things and step out of your comfort zone
- 👍 View challenges as opportunities to learn and improve, not as threats or obstacles
- 👍 Seek feedback and criticism as a way to identify your strengths and weaknesses and work on them
- 👍 Learn from the success of others and use them as role models and inspiration
- 👍 Praise yourself and others for the effort and process, not just the outcome
- 👍 Replace negative self-talk with positive affirmations and constructive questions

Celebrate your success, both big and small, in healthy and meaningful ways

Success is something that we all want and work hard for. It is a rewarding and satisfying feeling that **boosts our self-esteem and motivation.** However, sometimes we may forget to celebrate our successes, or we may celebrate them in unhealthy or unfulfilling ways. For example, we may-

- Neglect to acknowledge or appreciate our achievements and focus on the next goal
- Downplay or minimize our achievements and compare them with others
- Reward ourselves with unhealthy habits or indulgences that may harm our well-being
- Seek external validation or approval from others rather than from ourselves

These ways of celebrating success can diminish the value and joy of our achievements and make us feel dissatisfied or unhappy. They can also prevent us from learning from our success and using them as fuel for more value addition. To celebrate your success in healthy and meaningful ways, you can-

- Take time for self-care and relaxation, such as having a cup of coffee, a nap or meditation
- Spend time with your loved ones and share your achievements with them
- Show your appreciation and gratitude to the people who helped or supported you along the journey
- Be creative and express your success through art, music, writing, or any other form of expression
- Practice gratitude and reflect on what you have achieved and learned
- Do something fun and exciting that you enjoy
- Use your success as a motivation and inspiration for your next goal or challenge

Learn from Your Failures

Failure is something that we all **fear and avoid.** It is **a painful and disappointing**

feeling that lowers our self-esteem and motivation. However, failure is also inevitable in life. No matter how hard we try or how smart we are, **we will all experience failure at some point**. The person who has no experience of failure is the most inexperienced one. The question is, how do we deal with failure and learn from it? How do we turn failure into a stepping stone rather than a stumbling block?

The answer lies in **how we perceive and interpret failure.** If we see failure as a personal flaw or a permanent setback, we will feel hopeless and helpless. We will blame ourselves or others, make excuses, or give up. We will also miss the valuable lessons and insights that failure can offer us.

If we see failure as feedback or a temporary obstacle, we will feel hopeful and empowered. We will **take responsibility, analyze the causes, and find solutions.** We will also use the **failure as an opportunity to improve and grow.**

Failure is always a product of our uncontrolled emotions, cloudy imaginations, irrational assumptions, and diversified actions. This diversification is due to the superposition. Once you understand, tune, and channelize it through your clear vision, defined purpose, controlled emotions, natural feelings, rational assumptions, and focused actions, you succeed. This is all because of your ultimate position. Success lies somewhere between your superposition and your ultimate position.

As you can see, learning from failure can help you overcome the negative emotions and consequences of failure and turn it into a positive and productive experience. It can also help you enjoy the journey of manifesting your dream life, as you will see **every failure as a chance to get closer to your goal.** To learn from your failures, you can-

Accept and acknowledge your failure and the emotions that come with it

Reframe your failure as a learning experience, not as a personal defeat

Analyze your failure and identify what went wrong?

Find solutions and alternatives to overcome or avoid the same failure in the future

Seek feedback and advice from others who have faced or overcome similar failures

Implement the changes and improvements that you have learned from your failure

Try again and persist until you succeed

Sometimes it's advisable to **be resilient** enough to leave the stubborn attitude, change the mode of action, and re-analyze the whole process and purpose if necessary to achieve success. Failure is inevitable, but success matters.

Enjoy the Journey

Manifesting your dream life is not a destination, but a journey. It is not a one-time event, but a continuous process. It is not a linear path, but a dynamic and unpredictable adventure. Therefore, it is important to enjoy the journey and not just focus on the outcome. If you only care about the result, you may miss the beauty and joy of the journey. You may also feel frustrated or unhappy if you encounter delays or detours along the way.

To enjoy the journey of manifesting your dream life, you need to **be aware, grateful, and optimistic.** You need to-

Be aware and mindful of the moment, rather than dwelling on the past or worrying about the future

Be grateful and appreciative of what you have and what you have achieved, rather than complaining about what you lack or what you have not achieved

Be optimistic about the future, rather than pessimistic or fearful of the unknown

By staying aware, grateful, and optimistic, you will be able to enjoy the journey and experience more happiness and satisfaction. You will also be able to cope with the challenges and setbacks that you may face along the way. You will be able to celebrate your success, learn from your failures, and enjoy the journey of manifesting your dream life.

Conclusion

In this chapter, we have discussed how to celebrate your success, learn from your failures, and enjoy the journey of manifesting your dream life. We have explored how to adopt a growth mindset, celebrate your success in healthy and meaningful ways, learn from your failures and use them as opportunities for improvement, and enjoy the journey by being aware, grateful, and optimistic. By applying these strategies and tips, you will be able to achieve your goals and dreams, and more importantly, enjoy the process of achieving them. You will be able to manifest your dream life completely.

Keywords

- Creativity
- Creative Consciousness
- Dream Life
- Enjoy
- Fears
- Harmonic Alignment
- Infinite Intelligence
- Inner Harmony
- Joyful Growth
- Law of Attraction
- Law of Vibration
- Limiting Beliefs
- Manifestation
- Meditation
- Mindfulness
- Negative Patterns
- Neuroscience
- Quantum Mechanics
- Quantum Physics
- Quantum Self-awareness
- Spirituality
- Success
- Synchronicity
- Universal Law
- Universe Mind
- Universe Feedback
- Visualization